DAYDREAM ERRATICA

Kate Frances

ISBN: 978-1-915079-53-4

The author has asserted their right to be identified as the author of this Work in accordance with the Copyright, Designs and Patents Act 1988

Cover designed by Aaron Kent

Edited & Typeset by Aaron Kent

Broken Sleep Books Ltd
Rhydwen
Talgarreg
Ceredigion
SA44 4HB

Broken Sleep Books Ltd
Fair View
St Georges Road
Cornwall
PL26 7YH

Contents

Daydream Erratica

Kate Frances

that plane just flew
right over the sun
so shall I, too.

Figments

you, oh, you brief brigade
you bunting bodies
adorning the night
for a foothold to eternity.

and you –
cackling as a gaggle
to quiet the empire I –
but still the wooers wooing look
to anyone – smiling – cooing
cry, "we, the speckled sky" –
and straddling now, the endless now
the joyous and eternal now
go forth, and in your aerial nest
hatch your accidents.

now – yes – the lonely now
that nomad tale
who cleaving always leaves
free – a tireless I –
but then, yes!
you were divine
so damned divine
in brief.

Night Flight

in the wick-end
evening light
gather rat bouquets
blushing back
to the burrows
        against the night
                that   blue   hydra

take it
use it for a mug
an ashtray
a bathtub
shape the cackling blue
mould our cracking hydra –
take it

Hydra

roll me up
impress upon me that rhythm
that dances black and white
teach me to tuck myself
just right
so when I light
and the smoke is blue
as the geriatric day at the window
I can fly past lampshades
and the drifting window in your absence
to bury the name in the ashtray

Fixation

and Moon, You, noseying
the dark down of March
crinkling, weathered soft

soar, go, in fealty
carry the one – yes
folding me over

> do you feel
> the crest line
> up and over?

stride, carrying still,
still the same silk strait,
carouselling silent still

but nickering yes
and tethered taut
pearly chasing curve

Poise, seek praise
in the Lovers' sling
defy Goliath's night

> – none of this
arc above the jessamine, go,
feel it slip
repose in warmth
that must be branded yours
seared, or somesuch,
see?

toast up-raised
for carnal you
penned up gentle
soul-strung chords
blue and twisting
draping brassy down –
sigh whitely
and hold

Blues in Lunette

I'm still here
I'm still here
I am still
to the dirty rooted toe
here
if not to ride
empty-bellied
rolling under the
dumb dumb dumb
of streetlights

rising between
crystalised trees
rolling until the
dumb dumb stops
for stars, schooled,
curtsied to the field
act one, scene one,
for me and the whetted grass
stead fast
still

I'm Still Here

Wind, you must stop
fidgeting
do not bite your nails

your cradle home
is crawling vast
the squirrels are confused

Tree Tremor

.

bringing lemons to
the Green Hour
tiny – tarring – knots
full stops
playing braille
on the patio

the green green hour
glides on
the backstroke waltzed
small and circling full

the grey sky blushing
needs urgent repotting
its roots unwind from the bottom
Oh, great soft sprawl!
Mother Superior to the snails

The Green Hour With Ben

(Watercolour on Canvas)

voice and face: prescribed
in   settle   then out
          the ears again
cling   sullen
to a galloping garter
it's all breeze
          it chimes   signed
                    ash and ventriloquy

Ghost Hotel

unhinge your affections
make the darling case that you are not
Tuesday's Bombardier

in the death of diatribe
fire not your salute
lay down
            forget-me-nots

this is a soggy wretch
this it cannot answer you
not with such dishonoured faculty
not tarred so cold
to your tremors
to your tiny boars
            the pomegranate incise

don't thumb the tatters
with a loving touch
but, touching love, hold it –
limp and agonised
this cruelty and its frostbite brood
            shatter

Holepunch

I hold in my hand
Lady Satsuma

she has a glow to her
a flat-bellied weight
the sweetest dimples
stippling made
for the fingertips

the pieces of her
rounded thigh
crescent eye
fragrant hostels
for amnesiac glands
       for the nose
       a barbarian pop
       of redness, riding
       swooning
       on polyester
red has no place here
accosting this consecrated colour
orange is for worship

so, worship:
peel away, pretty veins
but keep the skin
smooth
it's too late
an afternoon
for sticky fingers
so:
prise open papal segments
tuck them in a box
go sit by a tree

she is with you
waiting
tilting the boughs
take out a segment
a curving crescent sigh
hold it to the light
see, she shimmers
and clutches it
in her humming core –
is the soul a thing to be touched?
a barbarian pop
orange this time
dribbling made
for the fingertips

if only you
were less like a moth –
but collisions stand
as murder at noon
orange is for murder
and

Lady Satsuma

and then the sound flew out of me
and I, remaining, fell
it sank in me
leviathan breeze
a breath spurned out in ecstasy

along my arching spine it flew
trembling with the starlight
the flash slipped out
so silently, a fanfare
for the flight of me

Cleared for Takeoff

and so it goes
off sets the fool –
but where?
      for milk?
what cause? for what
discord meaning trills
and ringing trips to pillage
      hatred, mine?

still the room
take the marks
capture it ejaculate
form desert ranks to
grit against the Rancid,
this State of the Turgid

but hate will deal
so, Lady, hold –
what? here, mercurial
and jingling too salty
to soft lay on the lips –
in petulance, it flourishes
      "what is your cause?"

      In magnus volley I
      defy what foolishness
      what bells you weld on me
      so shape me fool against myself –
      carve me from thy ribs

no more! although,
I am part fool
on my Father's side
and, wholly, on Sundays
it is a part –
and parts by nature

part the whole
and I, Magpie,
make collages –
as diligent as you
Reductor, as you set out
your circus dolls, who
in loyalty return
your designations –
swinging bludgeon
scornful blue
with some part clefting love
to mirror you

yes, Cloud Mountains
in dark little hats
broad angels in stillness
bare the white
of terror – how
tinted lilac luminaries
do you inform
the hating half of memory?
watch the metol
dye the stills of love
so, be, love as it may
merry and traipsing
the dew on the bluebells
who, nodding, drive up
in dreams, redolent attendant
to the night –
then, elbows knocking
with the Vanguard, then
damp the humming Moon,
the bells are debrided
that staining part
            interred.

If anything outlives this circus
be it *DEATH*
TO THE RHYTHMIC OPIATES
spend your pennies on
your spawning shits
in spite it pays
pretty and vile – those
glittered deposits – may this
be the brick through your window
tolling in salutation
singing, the vengeful knoll
swinging giddy, yes against
tender flabbing boredom

> Rage, craggy despot of
> the sluggish
> need be quarried, be refined:
> grind the dust and salt the slug
> that gave you bells
> in its own image

The Fool's Manifesto

this wind
dances around the bottle's top
singing as she goes

this same wind
flies whistling feathered kites
in sunny ceremony

a wind came all this way
to stead, to cool,
atop the world –
unfurl the sun
come barren, too,
for company, crooning
so hoarsely chasing
the rook

Simeon

so spat
far foul of a pretty mouth
glancing fatal gold finities
so glinting flicked
from the grazes
and back
to its malice
spliced across the eyelids
from its barbarous flight

skip back
to the quietude
lock the door
where, knowing
the grey hermit day
lulling and suspended
will hold you
as a hermit does

but you
spine to spine
against my scrawling parade
form the felling axe
that, swinging, hymns
red raw and ravaged
the fall

Spat

a dawning lawn
is set for tea
saucers by the sweet flat sea
see the mirror gentle sea
          "milk?"
no   "and sugar?"

but then,
these teaparty tourists
          love, did the deed
          with apathy
          amongst the cakes
          and the teaspoons
they will not topple their host
surely, cannot?

but then, there is Earl
dripping on the tablecloth
that drip, drip,
copulating drip

gaze nudge back
to a winded sea
knocked to the sternum
dropped
to a millpond mirror
pour tea down
to your understudy
and although the wind
for winding wound up gone
pancakes and paper
live in their flatness
and stir their joy

but then, considerations
dripped upon
ripple for the shore
and that drip
              drip
that copulating drip
in petulant all
wears holes in the carpet

Mirror Piece

there are thieves for intangible things
stealing and dealing in violence
burn them all
take it all back
with napalm

broad and tarry brush
neglecting circumstance for
devils, burned perversion
suited scabby in pinstripe
scratched in alabaster

burn, scraggles
Michelin-charred
      melt off the bones
      apply butter whilst hot

Empirical

there is only this minute
to trace the afternoon
        Friday afternoon
        sunny, warm
        March
from the bus
sailing through
check the little
café for yes, that
lanky form folded
head to the heels
sweeping, a discharged lover
a glimpse, a curl
in brief flops down
always your trousers are too short
too tall for– gone
and rolling on
past the pamphlet man who
is only young, familiar, maybe
the pub, charming
outstretched and rehearsed
but see
the tiny tapping foot betrays
the sapial condition– gone
gliding under the
sunny chimney stripes
an old lover's lover
she is sour and worried
– and gone

and to home
to the remnants
of visitors loved
vacated ships bound
for the busy afternoon
still, little lighthouse

sit inside me –
friends beck and
the lager smell
in heat
calls sweet in nauseous tones

but drop traces
craft the absence, yes
in the perfume that falls
and fades at the feet
of the carpet
the rucksack, the panties,
the lipstick branding
on the little half-glass—
fertilising love
and shaping the wake
– now, truly, gone

Friday Chronicle

twisting baby crimson
ribbons to your fingers
threadbare sodden from
contortion
touch the wake
a falling thing
a parasitic oily thing
a study of pain in spores
and flush.

Expulsion

how do these bricks
makes shapes familiar
make lines I know
to have noses in them
frowns I know to be loving?
mortar pleat a draft for me
show me   ruddy crumpled
show me   smiling eyes that
must I know must love me

Old Friends With Windows

we   lights strung up
all desperate to conceal
those halfformed hours
        perching lonely still
at a busstop
in a canyon
watching   warm   dogged
and fidgeting need
        chasing its tail
        desire undone
to time-signed cicada
        alone

Busstop Blues

and to think, now
of a twig that reaching would
if I stood still
take the temple
douse the old walks
in dregged ferment
ground under heel, already
       but, still, a man leans
       in a three-piece suit
       and a Spurs hat

Tragedy is gagging at
whatever floral wrought
this cannot stubborn be
because ticking little figures have
no consequence
for the bubbling draintop star
cough it upon
someone else

what comet does
our dear friend *he*
knot, and blushing, see?

thus, forage for no-one
and misdemeaning find
surprised – sit
in the lap of some other thing –
pine, sucking the hoo-ha palm
but, if, to lie in accord
only floundering then
might brace for chance
       may daffodils
       be lucky things
       for all the epithets

       they drink
       butter, soft and turning
       blink
layer, do your lying work
lie down, attend,
and dress, contend,
and dress these thicket vanities

Ground

Have you ever smelt
lavender after rain?
waltzing with the smoke
those minaret magnates
rivals dancing in the nonchalant light
of a fading, indifferent day

in this light
doubt is a melting thing –
the limp plague
dissipates, crawling
out from under fingernails
that cannot trace the lines
of love in rising
but fingers find redemption
thawed by the indigo scent
of forgiving November
patient November
more adorned in virtue than these
proud and dirty fingernails
who this morning punctured the
palms that could not coax
the ember bones

lather it up
under the mizzle
scrub hard enough and
all the disappointment will wash down the drain
the lumpy flesh-pilgrims
slipping down the skin
in pious succession
clean all the way down
to those rashy bones
itching in the night
and sick for the skin –

lather it,
until heavy white tears
run   down   the drain
vicious and viscous
run to meet the fishes
deserting the dirty fingernails

Shower Thoughts

Impotence arrives again
on horseback
with the papers
and Sunday Mist in Eagerness
brings the morning fog
to watch

blank apart and dancing –
chasing light-trails
not today
so falter lightly pirouette
dance to conceive
to grasp alone
pay no mind to the pandering lights

verses fail devotedly
words slumping in attention
to falling rust—
        look sharp, wee fish!
it something, falling dumb
whistling obstinate brick
diving, grinning
greet the sea
        fly for me, unresolved

Sploosh

what is this
name? this face? this
familiar shape
to a stranger
but strange
the shape of the sounds
well-worn –
this?
but love
to a lover?

what is the fox
without fable?

and this –
this intimate mutant?
mirrored and gazing
as everyday –
glossed over
and nothing like my charge
waiting
unmarked and so
joyfully estranged

and my name – to me –
the roundest lunar pebble
simmered down to the sound
the tongue to the teeth
of another
not mine
but a flash in the wings
the title of my portrait

oh, to greet the smallest hours
a nameless,
faceless thing
unworthy of the title 'thing'
to hear the toll and
catch myself
a stranger –
to know something
impossibly
for its dark and steaming self
freed across the tabletop
outlawed from its brittle skin
to sprawl and to stain
unkempt –
unspeakable, intangible
to know a Nothing –
          well –
to know impossibly

Even Nothing Has a Name

sun yourself
you pink turning bellies
you half-way, slender things
pick petals off a butter cup
with sticky fingers

yellow lady bugs
still flatten red
still smatter rhubarb-custard

speckle burning bellies
char, terrain of the idle
thus, crinkle curves and
cinders curl
blooming black in August

Bank Holiday

clamour call without you
certainty to the four-eight
tiny toe starlings
sweet puppeteers of
the two-step   my
         carotid rocket
         the alligator
rolling upwards
with victim rhythms
is missing

Out on the Town

standing against this litany
this first vomitus
of man
that contaminant of lunchtime
you will not know happiness

but then, some loves
have caves in them
some, with sardines,
beg you play the seal
at Calais
             feed me sardines
lie, loved ones, clapping

but Prince winked at you
in LAX
where happiness
strolled nearby
and nobody knew either of you

this sagging city
drooping damp
this crook-necked chicken
a hovel to impulsion –
feed me love
and feeling
knock back love
and feeling
go forth only
with love
and feeling

Steve's Biography

Kate Frances would like to thank David, Keston, her mother, and every friend who encouraged this work with kindness and pints.

'Spat' and 'Busstop Blues' were first published in *Fatberg*.

Acknowledgements

LAY OUT YOUR UNREST

www.ingramcontent.com/pod-product-compliance
Lightning Source LLC
Chambersburg PA
CBHW031634040426
42452CB00007B/830